Say It in Spanish

RescueLogic Speaks Your Language

Keywords and Phrases for a Bilingual RescueLogic System

Cadgraphics Incorporated
Makers of RescueLogic Software for Fire and Security Systems

"Safety Made Simple"

PO Box 11737
St. Paul, MN 55111-0737

Website: www.rescuelogic.com
Email: info@rescuelogic.com
Phone: (612) 722-3233

English phrases compiled by Dan Horon
Translated into Spanish by Maria Teresa Rojas

ISBN 978-0692241370

Table of Contents

Download a Microsoft Word version of this guide at RescueLogic.com, and you can cut and paste individual entries into your RescueLogic system.

RescueLogic is "Safety Made Simple."

Say It in Spanish

In an emergency, you need to communicate clearly with your safety and security team. If they speak Spanish, your RescueLogic system should, too.

This book can help. It includes hundreds of Spanish words and phrases — so you can add Spanish labels to your RescueLogic maps and floor plans, and Spanish "Take Action" messages to your emergency instructions.

Say It in Spanish lists terms that are commonly used in fire, security, and facility management. They're categorized by type, and listed in three sections; you'll probably refer to each section in order.

1. Floor Plan, Blueprint, and CAD Labels: Consult this section when you're labeling your maps and floor plans.
2. Fire and Security Keywords: Try these suggestions when you're setting up your fire and security systems.
3. "Take Action" Messages: Use these words and phrases as you compose your emergency "Take Action" instructions.

Each section is arranged alphabetically, with English words and phrases followed by their Spanish translation. Simply locate the words or phrases you need and enter them into your database.

With RescueLogic, safety truly is *simplificada*.

Map and Floor Plan Labels

Consult this list as you label your background maps and floor plans.

Access
Acceso

Air Conditioner
Aire Acondicionado

Area
Patio

Atrium
Atrio

Attic
Ático

Audio-Visual Room
Salón de Audio-Visuales

Auditorium
Auditorio

Baggage Claim
Reclamo de Equipaje

Balcony
Balcón

Basement
Sótano

Bathroom
Baño

Battery Room
Cuarto de Baterías

Bedroom
Alcoba

Break Room
Sala de Descanso

Building
Edificio

Business Office
Oficina de Negocios

Bypass
Bipás

Cafeteria
Cafetería

Campus
Ciudad Universitaria

Ceiling
Cielo Raso

Center
Centro

Changing Room
Salón de Cambio

Checkpoint
Punto de Inspección

Chiller
Enfriador

Classroom
Aula de Clases

Closet
Armario

Coat Room
Guardarropa

Command Center
Centro de Mando

Common Area
Área Común

Communications Room
Sala de Comunicaciones

Computer Area
Área de Computadores

Computer Room
Sala de Computadores

Concourse
Vestíbulo

Conference Area
Area de Conferencias

Conference Room
Salón de Conferencias

Control Room
Sala de Control

Copy/Fax Room
Sala de Copia/Fax

Corridor
Corredor

Courtyard
Patio

Critical
Crítico

Customer Service
Servicio al Cliente

Darkroom
Cuarto Oscuro

Data Center
Centro de Datos

Dining Room
Comedor

Directions/ North, South, East, West
Direcciones/ Norte, Sur, Este, Oeste

Directions/ Northeast, Northwest, Southeast, Southwest
Direcciones/ Noreste, Noroeste, Sureste, Suroeste

Display Area
Área de Exhibición

Dock
Muelle

Doctor's Office
Oficina del Doctor

Door
Puerta

Dressing Room
Cuarto de Vestir

Duct
Conducto

East
Este

Electrical Room
Cuatro Eléctrico

Elevator
Ascensor

Emergency Exit
Salida de Emergencia

Emergency Room
Cuarto de Emergencia

Employee Lounge
Sala de Empleados

Enclosure
Recinto

Entrance
Entrada

Entry
Entrada

Equipment Room
Cuarto de Equipos y Materiales

Escalator
Escalera Móvil

Exam Room
Salón de Exámenes

Executive
Ejecutivo

Executive Restroom
Baño de Ejecutivos

Exercise Room
Salón de Ejercicios

Exit
Salida

Eye Wash Station
Estación de Lavado de Ojos

Facility
Facilidad

Fence
Cerca

Fiber Optic
Fibra Óptica

Firefighter's Phone
Teléfono de Bomberos

Floor
Piso

Floors/ First, Second, Third, Fourth, Fifth, Sixth, Seventh, Eighth, Ninth, Tenth
Pisos/ Primero, Segundo, Tercero, Cuarto, Quinto, Sexto, Séptimo, Octavo, Noveno, Décimo

Freezer
Congelador

Furnace
Horno

Gallery
Galería

Garage
Garaje

Gate
Puerta

Generator
Generador

Greenhouse
Invernadero

Guard Station
Estación de Guardia

Gymnasium
Gimnasio

Hall (Large room)
Sala

Hall (Corridor)
Pasillo

Handicap Access
Acceso para Minusválidos

Headquarters
Sede Central

High-Security Area
Área de Alta Seguridad

Hot Tub
Baño Caliente

Information Desk
Recepción

Janitor's Closet
Armario del Conserje

Kiosk
Quiosco

Kitchen
Cocina

Laboratory
Laboratorio

Landing
Aterrizaje

Laundry Room
Cuarto de Lavandería

Level
Nivel

Library
Biblioteca

Light
Luz

Lobby
Lobby

Locker Room
Vestuario

Loft
Desván

Lounge
Sala (de estar)

Lower Level
Nivel Inferior

Luggage Area
Área de Equipaje

Machine Shop
Taller de Maquinaria

Mail Room
Salón de Correo

Mechanical Room
Salón de Mecánica

Men's Restroom
Baño para Hombres

North
Norte

Northeast
Noreste

Northwest
Noroeste

Nursery
Guardería Infantil

Nurses Station
Estación de Enfermería

Off Limits
Fuera de Límites

Office
Oficina

Open Area
Área Abierta

Parking
Estacionamiento

Pay Phone
Teléfono Público

Pool
Estanque

Press Room
Sala de Prensa

Private
Privado

Public
Público

Public Address System
Sistema Amplificador para Discursos Públicos

Pump
Bomba

Pump Room
Cuarto de Bombas

Quadrant
Cuadrante

Receiving
Recibir

Reception Area
Área de Recepción

Reception Desk
Recepción

Reception Room
Sala de Recepción

Recreation Room
Salón de Recreación

Recycling Station
Estación de Reciclaje

Refrigerator
Nevera

Restricted
Restringido

Restroom
Baño

Revolving Door
Puerta Giratoria

Roof
Techo

Room
Habitación

Sauna
Sauna

Security Room
Cuarto de Seguridad

Shipping
Embarque

Shipping and Receiving
Embarque y Recepción

Shop
Tienda

Shower
Ducha

Shutoff Valve
Válvula de Cierre

Solarium
Solana

South
Sur

Southeast
Sureste

Southwest
Suroeste

Sprinkler Room
Extintor de Incendios

Staff Lounge
Salón del Personal

Stairwell
Hueco de Escalera

Station
Estación

Storage
Almacenaje

Store
Tienda

Studio
Estudio

Sub-Basement
Subsótano

Subfloor
Subpiso

Sunroom
Solana

Supply Closet
Armario de Suministros

Swimming Pool
Piscina

Switch
Interruptor

Switchboard
Conmutador

System
Sistema

Tech
Técnico

Telephone
Teléfono

Telephone Room
Cabina Telefónica

Termination Closet
Armario de Terminación

Tower
Torre

Trash
Basura

Upper Level
Nivel Superior

UPS (Uninterruptable Power Supply) Room
Cuarto de UPS (Suministro de Energía Ininterrumpible)

Vending Machines
Máquinas de Comida Rápida

Vent
Rejilla (de Ventilación)

Vestibule
Vestíbulo

Waiting Room
Sala de Espera

Wall
Pared

Warehouse
Depósito

Water Heater
Calentador de Agua

West
Oeste

Window
Ventana

Wing
Ala

Women's Restroom
Baño de Mujeres

Work Area
Área de Trabajo

Workstation
Estación de Trabajo

X-ray
Rayos X

Yard
Patio

Fire and Security Keywords

Use these keywords for your fire and security stations.

Access Card
Tarjeta de Acceso

Air Conditioner
Aire Acondicionado

Alarm
Alarma

Alert
Alerta

Ambulance
Ambulancia

Armed/Disarmed
Armado/Desarmado

Backup Power
Energía de Reserva

Battery
Batería

Biohazard
Bioriesgo

Carbon Dioxide (CO2)
Dióxido de Carbono

Chemicals
Químicos

Climate Control
Control del Clima

Control
Control

Control Room
Sala de Control

Coolant
Líquido Refrigerador

Danger
Peligro

Dangerous Chemicals
Químicos Peligrosos

Dangerous Gas
Gas Peligroso

Dehumidifier
Deshumedecedor

Detector
Detector

Device
Mecanismo

Disabled
Inhabilitado

Emergency
Emergencia

Enabled
Habilitado

Evacuate
Evacuar

Explosive
Explosivo

Explosive Gas
Gas Explosivo

Extinguisher
Extintor

Extremely Flammable
Altamente Inflamable

Eye Wash Station
Estación de Lavado de Ojos

Fault
Avería

Fire
Fuego

Fire Alarm
Alarma de Fuego

Firefighter
Bombero

Flammable
Inflamable

Floor Plan
Planta

Furnace
Horno

Gas
Gas

Hazardous Materials
Materiales Peligrosos

Heat
Calor

Heat Detector
Detector de Calor

Heat Sensor
Sensor de Calor

High Temperature
Temperatura Alta

Humidifier
Hemedecedor

Hydrogen Gas
Gas de Hidrógeno

Immediately
Inmediatamente

Intruder Alarm
Alarma contra Intrusos

Ion Detector
Detector de Iones

Loss of Power
Pérdida de Energía

Low Battery
Batería Baja

Low Temperature
Temperatura Baja

Man Trap
Trampa de Hombres

Manual Station
Estación Manual

Map
Mapa

Motion Alarm
Alarma de Movimiento

Motion Sensor
Sensor de Movimiento

Natural Gas
Gas Natural

Needs Service
Servicio de Necesidades

On/Off
Prendido/Apagado

Photo Detector
Fotodetector

Police
Policía

Power Off
Apagado

Power On
Prendido

Propane
Propano

Protected Area/Unprotected Area
Crea Protegida/Área Desprotegida

Pull Station
Estación de Arranque

Pump
Bomba

Radiation
Radiación

Radioactive
Radiactivo

Security
Seguridad

Shut-Off Valve
Válvula de Cierre

Smoke
Humo

Smoke Detector
Detector de Humo

Sprinkler
Extintor

Sprinkler Shut-Off Valve
Válvula de Cierre de Extintores

Sprinkler System
Instalación de Rociadura Automática (para Extinción de Incendios)

Sprinkler Water Flow
Flujo de Agua para Extinción de Incendios

Strobe Light
Luz Estroboscópica

Supervisor
Supervisor

System
Sistema

Tamper Switch
Interruptor de Apretar

Tank
Tanque

Temperature Control
Control de Temperatura

Temperature-Controlled
Temperatura Controlada

Trouble
Problema

Unprotected Area
Área Desprotegida

Vent
Rejilla (de ventilación)

Water Leak
Escape de Agua

Water-Flow Switch
Interruptor de Flujo de Agua

Wire
Cable

Zoom In
Acercarse

Zoom Out
Alejarse

"Take Action" Suggestions

Use these words and phrases as you compose your "Take Action" emergency instructions.

A burglary may be in progress.
Puede estar llevándose a cabo un robo.

A chemical spill may be in progress.
Puede haber un derrame de químico.

A toxic leak may be in progress.
Puede haber una fuga de material tóxico.

Be prepared to use the fire extinguisher.
Esté preparado para usar el extintor de fuego.

Bring a flashlight.
Traiga una linterna.

Call [name] at [555-1212].
Llame a [Nombre] al [555-1212].

Call 911 for a hazardous materials team.
Llame al 911 y pida un equipo contra materiales peligrosos.

Call 911 for an ambulance.
Llame al 911 y pida una ambulancia.

Call 911 for the fire department.
Llame al 911 solicitando los bomberos.

Call 911 for the police.
Llame al 911 solicitando la policía.

Call 911 immediately.
Llame al 911 inmediatamente.

Call a supervisor.
Llame a un supervisor.

Call the building manager.
Llame al administrador del edificio.

Call the electric company.
Llame a la empresa de energía.

Call the gas company.
Llame a la compañía de gas.

Call the head of security.
Llame al jefe de seguridad.

Call the maintenance department.
Llame al departamento de mantenimiento.

Call the service company.
Llame a la compañía de servicios.

Call the telephone company.
Llame a la compañía de teléfonos.

Clear the area.
Despeje el área.

Close all doors and windows.
Cierre todas las puertas y ventanas.

Close all doors.
Cierre todas las puertas.

Close all windows.
Cierre todas las ventanas.

CO2 is deadly.
El CO2 es mortal.

Danger!
¡Peligro!

Do not attempt to handle this emergency alone.
No intente manejar solo esta emergencia.

Do not enter the area.
No entre al área.

Do not forget ...
No olvide...

Do not reset this alarm.
No engaste de nuevo esta alarma.

Follow the procedures for this condition.
Siga los procedimientos para esta condición.

Go to ...
Vaya a...

Go with a partner.
Vaya con un compañero.

Hydrogen gas is explosive.
El gas de hidrógeno es explosivo.

If you have determined that this is a false alarm that needs service, call _____.
Si ha determinado que ésta es una falsa alarma que necesita servicio, llame a _____.

Investigate.
Investigue.

Make sure all doors are locked.
Asegúrese que todas las puertas estén cerradas con llave.

Make sure everyone has left the area.
Asegúrese que todos han salido del área.

Make sure everyone has left the building.
Asegúrese que todos han salido del edificio.

[Name] has been called automatically.
[Nombre] ha sido llamado automáticamente.

[Name] is disabled and needs help to leave the area.
[Nombre] es minusválido y necesita ayuda para salir del área.

Re-arm the system.
Arme de nuevo el sistema.

Remember ...
Recuerde ...

Re-set the system.
Reconfigure el sistema.

Respond immediately.
Responda inmediatamente.

Secure the building.
Asegure el edificio.

Shut off the gas.
Cierre el gas.

Shut off the water.
Cierre el agua.

Someone has activated an alarm.
Alguien ha activado una alarma.

Steps
First, Second, Third ...
Pasos
Primero, segundo, tercero...

System malfunction.
Mal funcionamiento del sistema.

Take action.
Haga algo.

The _____ needs immediate attention.
El (la) _____ necesita atención inmediata.

The area is not protected.
El área no está protegida.

The area is protected.
El área está protegida.

The battery needs to be replaced.
La batería necesita ser reemplazada.

The door is closed.
La puerta está cerrada.

The door is locked.
La puerta está asegurada con llave.

The door is open.
La puerta está abierta.

The door is unlocked.
La puerta no está cerrada con llave.

The equipment may be malfunctioning.
El equipo puede estar funcionando mal.

The heat detector has sensed fire.
El detector de calor ha detectado fuego.

The motion detector has sensed activity in the area.
El detector de movimiento ha descubierto actividad en el área.

The power has been cut off.
La fuente de energía ha sido cortada.

The situation may be extremely dangerous.
La situación puede ser muy peligrosa.

The smoke alarm has sensed smoke.
La alarma de humo ha detectado humo.

The smoke detector has sensed smoke.
El detector de humo ha detectado humo.

The system is armed.
El sistema está armado.

The system is not armed.
El sistema no está armado.

The temperature is not within normal range.
La temperatura no está dentro del rango normal.

The temperature is within normal range.
La temperatura está dentro del rango normal.

There is a high risk of explosion.
Hay un alto riesgo de explosión.

There may be a fire.
Puede haber fuego.

There may be a leak.
Puede haber una fuga.

There may have been an explosion.
Puede haber ocurrido una explosión.

This is a drill.
Este es un ejercicio.

This is not a drill.
Este no es un ejercicio.

This is a test/This is not a test.
Esta es una prueba/Esta no es una prueba.

This is a true emergency.
Esta es una emergencia real.

Tune your radio to channel "x."
Sintonice su radio en el canal "x."

Use caution.
Sea cauteloso.

Wait for _____ to re-set this alarm.
Espere a _____ para reajustar esta alarma.

Wait for the hazardous materials team to arrive.
Espere a que llegue el equipo contra materiales peligrosos.

Wear a gas mask.
Use una máscara antigás.

Wear gloves.
Use guantes.

Wear protective gear: gloves, glasses, gas mask.
Use equipo protector: Guantes, gafas, máscara antigás.

Wear safety glasses.
Use gafas de seguridad.

Copyright Information

Patent Information

Cadgraphics and RescueLogic techniques and technology are protected by United States Patents 6,229,429 and 6,369,695.

Trademark Information

Disclaimer

The System Watch Handbook

The System Watch handbook introduces RescueLogic to the users who need it most: your site's security guards, emergency dispatchers, and first responders. At just 21 pages, it's a quick and easy read — and it's fully illustrated, in color.

Configure a MOXA Device

A MOXA Device — an NPort serial device server — makes it easy to connect your alarm panels to an Ethernet network so you can monitor them with RescueLogic® software. This technical bulletin shows you how to configure your device.

Get your copy at RescueLogic.com

Made in the USA
Monee, IL
04 November 2026

67384276R00015